MICHAEL BONILLA, CPCU, ARM

NEVER $ELL ON PRICE

An Insurance Agent Guidebook to developing a Consultative Sales Process for Auto and Home Insurance.

Never Sell on Price: An Insurance Agent Guidebook to developing a Consultative Sales Process for Auto and Home Insurance.

Book Information

Page Count: 123

Word Count: 14406

Author: Michael Bonilla

Publisher: Independently Published

Date Published: 1/15/2024

Title: Never Sell on Price: An Insurance Agent Guidebook to developing a Consultative Sales Process for Auto and Home Insurance.

Font Size: 12

Font Type: Calibri

Approximate Time to Read: 1-2 Hours

Copyright: United States of America

Format: Paperback, Kindle, Hardcover and Audible.

About the Author

Believe it or not this section is always the hardest for me to write about. I really don't enjoy talking about myself. I enjoy having people talk about themselves. What do people want to know about an author? Background? Experiences? Belief systems? I enjoy breaking things and putting them back together. What kind of person am I? What kind of person do I want to represent?

Let me tell you a brief story that tells you what kind of person I am. Back in the 90's I was sketching out my design for a pinewood derby car for boy scouts. This was my first race and I couldn't think of the type of car I wanted to build. To say the least there was zero inspiration. I scribbled out some designs on this piece of paper and eventually after running out of paper went into the den to find more paper. I stopped for a second and glanced over by the window. After staring out of the window for a second (maybe several minutes) I saw my father as he was pulling into the driveway with his 1990 White Dodge diesel, you could hear it for miles.

Then it hit me. What if I used his truck as the design? I re-read the

instructions and rules for the derby. The boxcar kit came in a small

cardboard box with a block of wood we could use to make our cars.

The instructions read as follows:

- Must have 4 wheels

- Must weigh X LBs, no more and no less.

- Must be X inches long by X Inches wide.

So, that being said. Nowhere in the rules/instructions did it

specifically say "this boxcar must be a car". So, for the first time in

the boxcar derby history. Michael Bonilla entered a truck. To which

everyone started laughing. It was a small wooded version of a

1990's Dodge Ram 2500. With a big Pepsi decal on the driver side

door. So, we called it the Pepsi truck.

I placed my 'car' on the race line for the first race and hoped for the

best. The judges looked at it. It met the weight requirements, the

size requirements and had the appropriate amount of wheels. So,

we raced and I waited with anticipation for the results. As I was short I couldn't even see the race. All I heard was, "Pepsi truck 1st place." After all 5 races that day I kept hearing those same words over and over again.

After sweeping that year's event. The following year I decided to change it up and make a replica of the Mach 5 Speed Racer Car, in which I came in third place. That next year every 'car' was a truck, besides mine. Don't bend the rules, don't break the rules, test the rules and test the boundaries of the game you are given. Look for loopholes and exploits in the system.

I'm unsure what kind of insight that might have provided. Nevertheless, this book is the longest, most through and probably well thought out I have written to date. I'm an author, a consultant, a former agency owner, an avid golfer, a husband and most importantly someone who enjoys giving back through teaching.

PINEWOOD DERBY CONTEST
"1ST PLACE WINNER" 1997

Table of Contents

"People are afraid of things they don't understand. They don't know how to relate. It threatens their security, their existence, their career, image." -Bill Laswell

Introduction

There is no such thing as a good deal for the wrong insurance policy. Yet, why is it that *so* many people have the wrong insurance? The biggest problem facing consumers in the insurance market is what? What is it? <u>Consumers understand what they are paying for insurance, but they don't understand what they are actually paying for.</u> The reality of purchasing insurance in America is that people do not fundamentally understand what they are purchasing. *96%* of drivers misunderstand at least one key aspect of their car insurance policy, and more than half have false assumptions about multiple features of their coverage (Vohra, 2022).

Think about that for a second. The best case with insurance is that you purchase insurance, pay for it until you die and hope you never have to use it. Yet, people will pay for something their entire life, and never truly understand it. That is unless, they have to actually use it, then they become veritable experts overnight.

If you ask most consumers about the insurance buying experience, they'll tell you a similar story.

- Insurance is hard to understand.

- Insurance isn't easy to purchase.

- Insurance is a necessary evil.

- Insurance is a headache.

- Insurance is frustrating to buy.

And frankly, I can't blame them for thinking that. If I went to shop for a product, and all anyone ever talked about was the price of that product, I'd probably think the same thing. In fact, before we all got into the industry, we probably thought something very similar. Let's talk about how to make insurance easy to buy for the consumer. What a novel concept, I know.

Your job is to make insurance relatable. How do we make it relatable? Education is the foundation to making people more comfortable in their buying decision and confident in you being their agent.

Have you ever 'secret shopped' one of your major competitors? If you're reading this book, there is a good chance that I have secret shopped you. For the better part of the past decade, I have been secret shopping about 2 insurance agents per week. You should try it some time, the results might shock you. Most Agents, call centers, anyone selling insurance will spend about 6 to 7 minutes of time with you on the phone. After you've answered enough questions they find a way to rush you off the phone and move on to the next call. How many questions do you think the average Insurance Sales Consultation has? 12 Questions. There's about 12 questions between me and a quote. Don't believe me, try it out some time.

Why should you 'never' sell on price?

I believe insurance has not become just another commodity. Insurance is not like a bar of soap, you can't just walk into a grocery store and pick it up off the shelf. Insurance is a serious financial instrument. When I say you should 'never sell on price', I mean you should never have to rely on it solely as a selling strategy. If you need to use your insurance one day, you won't care too much about your annual premium. I can tell you, you'll probably care a whole lot about whether or not you can use your insurance. Price is a trap. Most agents think their value stretches as far as the premium savings they can provide a client. You can never guarantee you'll be the cheapest policy, but you can guarantee how you sell your value as an agent.

Don't fall for the 'Price' fallacy!

If you talk to ten agents and ask them what consumers care about the most when buying insurance. What will they say? How will they answer that question. 9 out 10 will tell you Price is the only thing customers care about. And, I can't blame them. If ten customers walked up to me and asked me to lower their price, I might be convinced that the ONLY thing people care about is price. The truth is, if all people cared about was price, your retention rate would be 5% or 10%. So, what's happening? What's shaping our perspective? It's called the *Recency Bias*. Recency bias is a cognitive bias that causes individuals to more easily remember something that has happened recently.

The Importance of Agency Selling Standards

I believe buying Insurance shouldn't be a confrontational experience, it should be a collaboration between an Agent and a Consumer. It's crucially important that you design a sales process with that concept in mind. Part of that philosophy, I've always found, is anchored in having agency selling standards. What are standards? When someone comes to my agency, there is a standard minimum offering, there is a standard experience. I know they will walk away with and say X, Y and Z. Every successful business has strong standards and processes.

What's your favorite meal? Let's just say, it's a Hamburger. Are you confident that every time you order a Hamburger, the Hamburger will be the same? You have an expectation of what a Hamburger is, how it is made and what a Hamburger is not. What if you ordered a Hamburger and there was a fried piece of fish on top of the hamburger. What if you ordered it, and it was cut into 5 pieces? The reason you are confident in your order, is the fact that business has standards they adhere to when making a hamburger.

Principle #1: Never assume the Agent before me did their job correctly.

This was probably the most important principle, because it is the most dangerous assumption you can make as a salesperson. If I already know that 96% of people I speak with don't understand their insurance, then that allows me ample room to explain the coverage.

Principle #2: Never compare apples to apples.

If we know for a fact that most people do not understand their insurance, why in the world would you copy their current insurance policy and then recommend that same coverage back to them? If you went to a Doctor for a second opinion, and all that Doctor did was copy the First opinion, how would feel? You'd probably not feel too good about that opinion. The whole point of getting a second opinion is because you have doubt in the first opinion. Otherwise, you would have went with the first opinion.

Principle #3: It is not my job to spend the client's money for them.

The best Marketing Rep I ever had, his name was John, taught me an invaluable lesson. He worked for a company that had a competitive rating of 1% in the State. Meaning, the price was in the lowest 3 prices on a multi-rater 1% of the time. It was rarely ever the lowest price offering in the state, and for good reason. John came to our office one day and was, he was, fairly frank about our results with said company. He said, "What happened? When I got you guys appointed you said you would write a ton of business?" I can't say I blame him, because we didn't write that much with said company. I said, "John, I don't know what to tell you.

When we rate a Home policy with you guys, you're not even in left field, you're out of the ball park. Sometimes double the price. Sometimes more than double." I pulled up a recent quote and showed him the less expensive options. Now, at this early stage in my Insurance Agent career, I'll admit it, we sold on price, we didn't know any better.

But, everything changed for me after John came to my office that day. He said, "Mike, what's your point?" I said, "How can you expect me to pitch this to the client?" He then proceeded to ask me a question that shook me to the core, it changed my reality. He asked, "Whose job is it to spend the client's money?" To which I was dumbfounded. A lightbulb turned on in my head. He asked, "Do we offer the best or the worst coverage of those companies you have?" I said, "Probably the broadest of them all." To which he said, "there is a reason why we are more expensive. Sell the coverage, pitch it to the client, and see what they have to say. You'll always have a cheaper option in your back pocket."

How do people make decisions?

The Rational Decision-Making Process

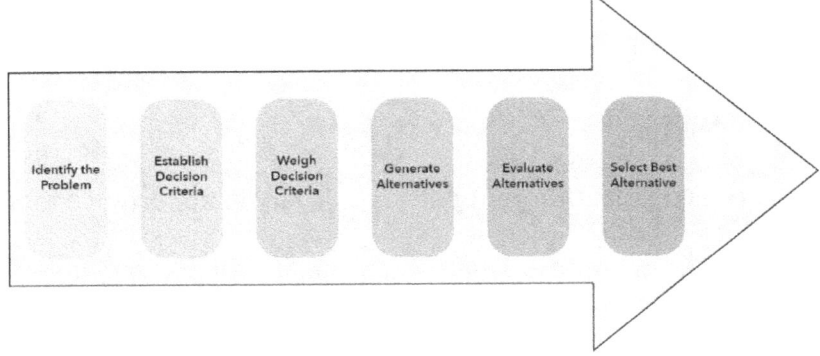

Max Bazerman defines the Rational Model of Decision Making as the following six step process:

1. **Define the Problem.** However, people often act without a thorough understanding of the problem to be solved, leading them to solve the wrong problem. Accurate judgment is required to identify and define the problem. People often err by (a) defining the problem in terms of a proposed solution, (b) missing a bigger problem, or (c) diagnosing the problem in terms of its symptoms. Your goal should be to solve the problem, not just eliminate its temporary symptoms.

2. **Identify the criteria.** Most decisions require you to accomplish more than one objective. When buying a car, you may want to maximize fuel economy and comfort while minimizing cost. The rational decision maker will identify all relevant criteria in the decision-making process.

3. **Weigh the criteria**. Different criteria will vary in importance to a decision maker. Rational decision makers will know the relative value they place on each of the criteria identified. The value may be specified in dollars, points, or whatever scoring system makes sense.

4. **Generate alternatives.** The fourth step in the decision-making process requires identification of possible courses of action. Decision makers often spend an inappropriate amount of time seeking alternatives. An optimal search continues only until the cost of the search outweighs the value of the added information.

5. **Rate each alternative on each criterion.** How well will each of the alternative solutions achieve each of the defined criteria? This is often the most difficult stage of the decision-making process, as it typically requires us to forecast future events. The rational decision maker carefully assesses the potential consequences of selecting each of the alternative solutions on each of the identified criteria.

6. **Compute the optimal decision.** Ideally, after all of the first five steps have been completed, the process of computing the optimal decision consists of (1) multiplying the ratings in step five by the weight of each criterion, (2) adding up the weighted ratings across all of the criteria for each alternative, and (3) choosing the solution with the highest sum of the weighted ratings.

System 1 and System 2 thinking

In most buying situations, we don't use a Rational model, we use an Emotional model. This is referred to as, "System 1 or System 2 Thinking". System 1 Thinking is considered the intuitive system of decision making. System 1 is fast, automatic, effortless, implicit and emotional. System 2 Thinking is the opposite of System 1. System 2 thinking involves reasoning that is slower, conscious, effortful, explicit and logical (Stanovich and West, 2000). So, what does insurance fall under? Is it System 1 or System 2? It depends on your sales process. If you have a 6-minute sales process (which is average) and only present on price. You force the person to make a snappy gut decision. People rely on system 1, when they are not empowered to use System 2.

How do Consumers Judge your sales Process?

When a customer speaks with you, plan on them asking two questions. Question 1: Did this person solve my problem? Question 2: How was my experience? We can break it down into this grid system below.

| | | Was my Problem Solved? | |
		Unsolved	Solved
How was my Experience?	Bad	B, U	B, S
	Good	G, U	G, S

Based on the above grid, there are effectively four options for a salesperson. You can produce a Bad experience, and not solve a problem. You can produce a Bad Experience and Solve the problem. You can have a good experience, but not solve the problem. You can have a Good Experience and Solve the problem.

Which aspect of the sales process is the most important outcome? Experience over solution. You always want the person to walk away with a good experience, because that can produce referrals. You **cannot** solve every customer problem all the time. You **can** focus on having a good experience speaking with you every time.

Designing a Sales Process – Where do I want to compete?

Can you reliably be the least expensive option on the market? What if you designed a process in mind that didn't rely on you being the cheapest option? That would be designing a process in reality. What if you assumed that you will be more expensive? What if you assumed you would be more expensive and offer more coverage? There are effectively 9 possible outcomes for a customer in your sales process.

	Less Expensive	Same Price	More Expensive
Less Coverage	Less for Less	Sames for Less	More for Less
Same Coverage	Less for Same	Same for Same	More for Same
More Coverage	Less for More	Same for More	More for More

Deciding where and when to compete is a crucial part of any strategic framework. When I was a new agent, I was rather desperate, so I chose to compete everywhere, all the time and under any circumstance. As I failed, and learned, I decided to sell on price, but narrow my focus. I decided to compete in the 'Less Expensive' column. This didn't last very long however, because ultimately I realized everyone and their brother was competing in the same spot. It was a crowded marketplace full of cut-throat Price Merchants and I decided to make a change. I decided to compete in the 'More Expensive' column and 'More Coverage' column, because there was almost **NO** competition.

Understand Your Audience

There are basically just two types of people in this world. There are what I call 'Think' people and there are 'Feel' people. Think people tend to be thinkers. They like Numbers, Factoids, Statistics, and Trivia. Think People tend to love visual aids that are data driven, charts, spreadsheets, etc. Feel people tend to be the exact opposite of Think people. They think with their feelings. Feel people love stories, anecdotes, customer testimonials, parables, and or hypothetical situations. Feel people tend to enjoy colorful and creative designs. Why does it matter? In 2020, a study found that **40.7%** of shoppers switched because ***"Feeling like you are not being treated fairly."*** It matters because not every customer will receive information in the same way, which means you need to read the room and make adjustments in real-time when selling to different types of clients.

Why might someone want to pay more for their insurance?

Why might someone want to pay more for their insurance? This is one of my most consistent opening questions when speaking to agents. I can think of one obvious reason, people are under-insured more often than not. I think we have the premise all wrong. People don't over-pay for insurance, people under-pay for insurance. There are dozens of reasons why someone might want to pay more for insurance and hopefully one of the reasons is **Y-O-U**. You, as a licensed insurance agent, can be the difference maker in someone's life. You can be the difference between what ends up being a bad day or a financially devastating day for a family.

One of our clients lost a son in a car accident. It was tragic. He was shipping off to the military academy on Monday, I believe the accident happened either Friday or Saturday night. He was driving a late 90's Honda, a rather small vehicle. From the Police Report, they were able to determine that the car probably lost control in the higher 80's lower 90's and propelled into a large tree. The car instantly was engulfed in flames.

Two days prior, when we sold the insurance. The Client had minimum limits for a number of years. We were able to up-sell the client on a few Optional Coverages. One of which being Medical Payment Coverage, which they never had before. This policy applied Med Pay to Death & Dismemberment up to a certain limit. We hand delivered the Med Pay check to cover the funeral expenses for his son. Nothing will indemnify him of that loss, but for a father who was impoverished at the time, that check was the difference between a funeral service or an urn for his son.

What we do as Insurance Agents is important. You have to fundamentally believe that. It's easy to lose sight of that. It's easy to think, "I just *sell* insurance." In fact, what we do is protect families and assets from the unknown. In my opinion, Insurance is the greatest Societal Good ever created.

Using Strategic Pausing

One of the most powerful tools a salesperson can use is the 'Strategic Pause'. It's an art to learn this, but very powerful once you do. Pausing does a couple of things. It gets the person engaged. Gets them to think. Gets them demonstrate relative comfortability or nervousness in the conversation. Tells me if they are paying attention or dozing off to sleep. Let your words simmer. Don't try to blurt out a flurry of important points. Take your time and let the person digest your points.

Transmute: Making the intangible into tangible

Insurance is an intangible product, which is why most people struggle selling it. As you build out your sales process, make it real to people. The easiest way to do that is by explaining the coverage and providing real world examples.

Telling Isn't Selling

There's an old sales Philosophy that states, "Telling Isn't Selling." Now, what does that mean to you? Here's what it means to me. It means you have two ears and one mouth. So, you need to listen twice as much as you speak. It means you need to ask questions. There's something sloshing around in your skull. It's called a brain. The only way to extract the information in your brain is by asking you questions. Questions are crucial to selling coverage. Why? Because, it takes informed consent in order to get people to pay more for something. People want to know what it is they are actually paying for, preferably before they pay for it. How many people like hanging around with someone who constantly tells them what to do? Doesn't sound very enjoyable to me. You can tell someone what to do until you are blue in the face, but selling an idea involves the other person making decisions. Our job is to educate, then make a professional recommendation and sell that recommendation. Education is the key to facilitating a comfortable buying experience for the client.

Note: Too many questions turns a Sales Consultation into a Sales Interrogation.

The 7-38-55 Rule

In an 'in-person' sales conversation, only **7%** of what you actually say is perceived by the client in how they interpret what you said. The '7-38-55' rule of communication basically is just that simple. When people interrupt what we say, only **7%** of it comes from the actual words themselves, **38%** from our Tonality and **55%** comes from our Body Language (See below Chart).

	In-Person	Over the Phone
Spoken Words	7%	15%
Voice / Tone	38%	85%
Body Language	55%	0%

The Q.E.R.C System

The Q.E.R.C System is a simple sales system I developed to build training wheels around how to sell products and coverage, mostly to sell concepts of Insurance.

Question: Ask a Question to get the Attention of the Insured.

Educate: Use their response to your Question as a chance to Educate.

Recommend: Make your professional recommendation based on their specific Needs.

Close: Close with a Question.

Never Assume, Ask.

A close Friend of mine was insured with a well-known Captive Insurer and I assumed he was taken care of by his Agent. Boy, was I wrong. For the sake of this story, let's call him Tom. One day, I asked Tom that I review his Insurance with Big Captive Co insurance Company. I assumed he had good coverage, because he was High-Net Worth. He owned a Million Dollar Condo, a Six-Figure Auto and a Second Vehicle that was mid-value. He was the only driver on the policy and had plenty of additional assets in the bank.

Tom and I met up at a coffee shop, and he brought his paperwork with him. As I was looking over the paperwork my jaw nearly dropped on the floor. The Agent sold him State Minimum limits, which in California come out to 15/30/5. His Condo had somewhere in the realm of 25% of the needed Property/Personal Belongings coverage with only $100,000 Liability. Granted, this conversation happened about ten years ago, but it went something like this...

Agent: Tom, you have State Minimum Limit Auto Coverage, do you know what that means?

Tom: Based on how you said that, I'm assuming that it is really bad.

Agent: Explained the coverage limitations.

Tom: Oh, boy...

Mind you, I only walked into the conversation expecting to review his adequate coverage and make some basic recommendations. I had Zero intention to sell him. Needless to say, after explaining the gaps in his coverage, he signed up with the next day.

Don't Fix Something That Ain't Broken.

Our job is to offer solutions, not to make up problems. A Loan Officer sent me a lead one day, with a Home Policy from a very large insurance company. The client wanted a quote. I told him that on the surface, the coverages were exactly what I would have quoted that client and he was probably better off just staying with his current agency, but should consider a higher deductible.

Develop an Underwriting Philosophy

An underwriting philosophy is a simple credo explaining how you underwrite. As a 'Field' underwriter, licensed agent, you are the first layer of defense for an insurance company. I had a relatively simple motto. I wanted to insure a client as well as I would insure my own grandmother. I wouldn't sell a policy that I wouldn't buy. If it were my money paying the claim, would I take the bet on that client.

Using *Non-Generic* language

I'll never forget my first Apartment Owner, Stef. Stef was insured with a large carrier that specialized in Habitational, but we had a good rapport and an existing client-relationship prior to me becoming an agent. I'll never forget it, because I offishly stumbled through writing my first Apartment Complex. It wasn't a large complex, or even that large of a policy, but for me every policy was large at the time.

I presented the coverage, up-sold some minor coverage differences, proposed a higher deductible as the building was older and would benefit greatly from the premium discount. It was more or less a slam dunk, because the carrier I represented at the time really wanted to get into the habitational market.

So I went in for the close, and foolishly said, "Most of my clients choose to go with a monthly payment plan, because of..." Mid-sentence Stef placed his hand gently on my wrist as I was jotting down numbers and said, "Michael... I'm not most of your clients. I'm me. Here's how I like to pay."

It was right there and then, I learned that I wasn't treating him like an individual, I was treating him like a number, like "one of my clients", not as a person. People like to feel unique, different, special, and most importantly heard. If you speak in generic terms, you get generic results. If you speak in specific terms, you get specific results.

Pre-Empt Objections, Don't Avoid Objectionable Things, Bring Them Up in advance of Your Proposal

Objections are best resolved before they occur. Most objections are predictable, because they are almost always the same. Bring up topics early that people tend to object to at the end of the process. Optional Coverages often get objected to, if you wait until the end to discuss them. There is a reason they are not mandated coverages, they are optional. A classic example might be Building Ordinance or Ordinance of Law on a Home Policy, or Medical Payment coverage for Auto insurance. How often do you hear, "I don't think I need that coverage?" If you hear it a lot, then it might be because of your process.

Planting the Seed of Doubt: What am I paying my current Agent for?

My mentor once told me, you need to plant the seed of doubt. That is what we sell. We sell fear of the unknown. An easy way to plant the seed of doubt, is throwing the current agent under the bus, in an ethical manner. When you sell based on exposing Gaps or identify Gaps in coverage, who sold that current gap-filled policy? The current Agent did. It is the job of an Agent to prevent those Gaps, and that creates a tremendous amount of value for you as an agent.

Here are some basic examples of what I mean.

Agent: John, has anyone ever bothered sitting down with you and explaining how your insurance is supposed to work?

Agent: John, when was the last time your current agent offered to sit down with you and explain your insurance?

Agent: John, when was the last time your current agent made sure your policy was up to date?

Agent: John, when was the last time your agent offered to review your insurance coverage needs?

"Slow is smooth, smooth is fast." Comfortable and Confident

There is a saying in the military, which I think is pertinent to selling, "Slow is smooth and smooth is fast." In essence, it means, you don't want to rush into doing the wrong things. There is no bigger L in life, than looking foolish after making a bad purchase. What we want to do in Consultative sales is empower consumers to make good purchasing decision on behalf of their family and assets. We do this by making them comfortable and confident. It's hard to be good at something you are not comfortable doing, when you understand something you gain confidence.

When should you deviate from a sales process?

A sales process is a science, but closing is more of an artform. A sales process can be a powerful tool, but you gotta learn when to turn it off. Don't be enslaved to your sales process. Knowing when to deviate from a sales process takes expertise, which means it takes practice and time. Your lead sources should also affect how you view your sales process. Some prospects are in a hurry and don't want to invest the time to talk about protecting their assets. I've always found people invest time in what they care about, so see if they care about their stuff. Making adjustments on the fly is probably the hardest skill to learn, but it is something worth learning, quickly.

Collaboration, not Confrontation

Consultative Selling is a collaboration, which involves empowering the consumer to make informed decisions. When using language, I tend to use 'we' a lot, to emphasis that this is a collaboration between two people. For example, "As your agent, here is what I recommend that WE do." Many people think that, 'if you speak first, you lose.' I think that if you disagree first, you lose, as a salesperson. If you want to disarm a prospect, be the first to agree.

Don't be flimsy with your Recommendation, be steadfast.

People can tell if you are wish-washy with your recommendations. People can also tell if you have integrity and stand behind your recommendation. If you make a recommendation, see what the client really has to say. When I was a younger Agent, I learned this the hard way. I made recommendations, and out of nervousness or cutting the silence I would talk my way out of a sale. One day, I invited a prospect to the office for a Quote/Proposal. Luckily, he provided me his Dec pages prior to the meeting and I was able to get a lot of the work done. He owned a home, had two autos with mid-tier coverage, a clean driving record, no umbrella policy and a good profession. On paper, he was a perfect client, but patently under-insured. I made my recommendation, which in essence was to sell higher deductibles, bundle and higher coverage. Mind you, this was about a decade ago, but I think we came in around 10% more expensive or just under 10%. He'd been insured with his company for nearly 5 years and hadn't shopped. So, I made the recommendation.

Agent: John, your Auto, Home and Umbrella policy comes out to X amount per month. How would you like to pay?

His eyes elevated slightly as I went in for the close. I handed him the proposal to look over, and I shut up. I'll never forget that sale, because of what happened next. I sat there and leaned in, and shut up. And, I shut up. A couple minutes went by, so I swiveled my chair slightly and pretended to fondle through some paperwork on my desk like I was doing something productive. A couple more minutes went by. My business partner who was on his computer in the same room even turned around in his chair to see if everything was okay. My business partner glanced over at me and I shot him a quick head nod. The prospect kept looking at my proposal and then back at me to see if I would say something. Man, I was cool as a cucumber. I stopped randomly looking at papers and then turned back to the client. We must have went dark for like ten minutes. He shook his head and said, "Let's do it."

What are we in the Business of doing?

We are in the insurance business. Yeah, but what is that? We are in the business of protecting families and assets. We are not in the business of *just* selling insurance policies. We protect families and assets, by selling them insurance. Insurance is just the vehicle to accomplish our mission.

Bring 1 in the front door, only to lose 2 out the back door.

Does it make sense to have a high closing sales process, if you have low retention? It depends on the agent and the lead source. For me, the name of the game of Retention. I wanted to find a way to sell to clients who had the lowest loss ratio and highest retention rate. Why? Two reasons.

- First, the insurance industry has the highest customer acquisition costs of any industry.

- Second, it costs seven to nine times more for an insurance agency to attract a new customer than to keep one.

So how do I find these clients? These clients tend to want to stay around at least 4 Renewals and Bundle 2+ policies with your agency. Why do I want a client to stick around at least 4 years? Research has shown that churn (customer defection) is at its highest **one year** after a customer purchases their first policy. It decreases significantly after **four** years (Agentero, 2024).

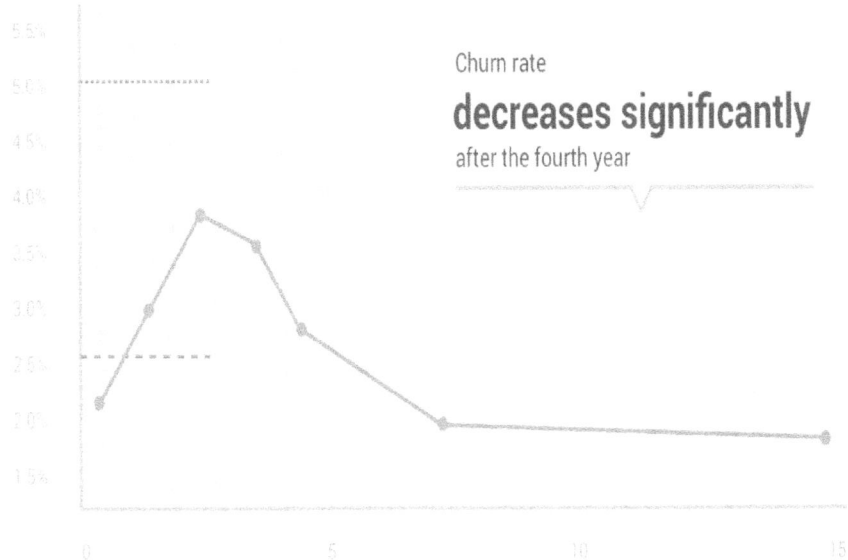

Further research by Arthur Middleton Hughes has demonstrated there is a direct correlation between the numbers of policies a client has and the retention rate of that client (See Chart Below).

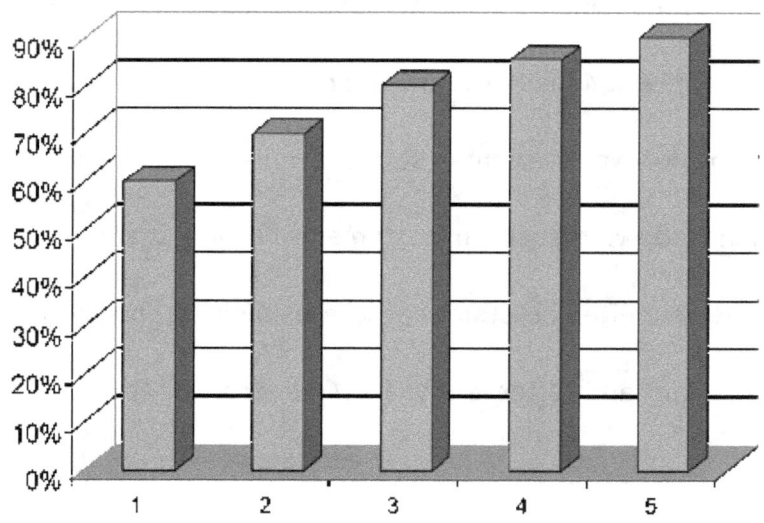

Retention rate based on the number of products owned.

Great minds discuss ideas. Average minds discuss events. Small minds discuss people. – Eleanor Roosevelt

How do we make Insurance Easy to buy? How do we make Insurance relatable?

First, we need to understand the perspective of the consumer. Consumers do not understand their insurance. If they don't understand their coverage, or how their insurance works, what do they focus on? They focus on the price. That doesn't mean they only care about price, it might be the only thing they can comprehend about their insurance policy.

Consumers only Care About Price, or Price is the #1 Reason people Shop/Switch

How often do Americans Comparison shop for auto insurance? In 2015, *Insurancequotes.com* commissioned a study conducted by Princeton University to answer this very question. The survey found that people shop;

- Multiple times Per Year: 7%

- Once A Year: 24%

- Ever Few Years or Never: 66%

- Other: 3%

Objectively, we can review Annual Reports from publicly traded insurance companies to figure this out. A preferred Auto Insurance carrier in the United States will have somewhere between a 90 to 95% first term renewal ratio for a six-month auto policy.

The question then becomes, if 33% of shoppers are shopping on a regular basis (once or more per year), then how can insurance companies maintain consistently high Retention rates? In a recent survey, 84% of drivers surveyed agreed the comparing car insurance quotes between multiple provides saved them money (Vohra, 2022).

Which begs the questions, if Price is **so** important, why do so few people shop and fewer yet actually end up switching insurance companies?

Furthermore, if we look at data from the Comparative Rating Companies we find the exact opposite of 'Price' switching. In fact, **57%** of consumers who call independent agencies do not take the lowest quote provided. Rather, they choose insurance that costs between **19%** and **53%** more than the lowest quote provided (Jans, 2016).

What Prompts a Consumer to Shop for Insurance?

Let's accept that Price is **a** primary reason in how we make buying decisions. In the United States, there are approximately **104,270** insurance commercials per year on television and radio (Spitznagel, 2022). Customers are constantly bombarded with insurance advertisements. In fact, American Auto insurers spent more than **$10 billion** on advertising in 2021. But, what effect has this had on the American Insurance Shopper? In a recent survey by JD Power it found that, the 30-day average shopping rate reached 13.1% in March 2023, the highest rate since June 2021 and well above the 2021 average of 11.4%.

We're they Non-Renewed?

In California, approximately 13% of the total voluntary homeowners and dwelling fire policies were non-renewed in 2021, compared to 11% in 2018 based on the number of policies reported in each year (California Department of Insurance, 2022). Non-Renewals are a significant driver of shopping, but have very little to do with the **P** word. Effectively, based on these statistics alone, for California, 1 out of 9 shoppers were purely looking for insurance out of necessity not necessarily price.

Lapse in Coverage, Cancellation

Unfortunately, it is nearly impossible to quantify the Lapse Ratio for our industry based on any publicly available data sources. So, we have to turn to surveys. In a recent survey by TransUnion, a global information and insights company, the survey found nearly 15% of consumers owned or used a vehicle without valid coverage or had allowed their coverage to lapse within the past six months. That's approximately 1 out of 7 Auto insurance clients lapsing coverage. For additional context, *this survey was conducted for customers with Credit Scores ranging from 300 to 500, which on average have a higher-than-normal lapse ratio.*

Did they Lose their Agent?

In 2022, the estimated total number of independent property-casualty agents and brokers in the U.S. stands at 40,000, an increase from 36,000 in 2020. NAMIC says over the next 15 years, 50% of the current insurance workforce will retire. This will leave more than 400,000 open positions unfilled, while less than 25% of the industry is under the age of 35. I received a Homeowners quote request from a Loan Officer one day. The policy looked fine, and I was prepared to just tell him to stay with his carrier.

That is until, until, I noticed something. The Homeowners policy didn't have a Multi-policy discount, but was located in a very nice part of Ventura County. So, I pinged the Loan Officer and asked if I could meet with the client, if he had any other insurance. He said, 'funny you mention it, he wants to meet with you.'

When I arrived at his home, I noticed a rather large Recreational Vehicle in the driveway and two other vehicles. He invited me in and we sat down at the kitchen table. We did the usual chit-chat and he went over to a desk and pulled out 6 manilla file folders. Each was labeled 'Insurance'. Here's what I found. He plopped them down and I started dissecting them. He had a Personal Auto with Big Captive Carrier. He had a Motorhome policy with Large Direct Internet insuer.com. He had a Home policy with well-known large Home insurer. He had an Earthquake Policy. He had an umbrella policy. He had a Landlord policy. Know what all those policies had in common? His name. That's it. He had 6 policies with 6 different agents and insurance companies. You're a smart person, obviously I know that because you're reading this book. As a smart person, why do you think someone would do such a thing? Why would someone pay 6 different bills to 6 different insurance companies and 6 different agents?

Pirce? That's what I thought at first. What happened to this customer, is time. He was around 90 or so, when I insured him with one company. I asked him a simple question, "Bob, would you consider paying slightly more for your insurance if I could put it all in one spot?" He said, maybe. See, for Bob, Time had passed him by. He had a 75-year-insurance-history. What does that mean? It means that 75 years ago he bought a policy. He outlived his agent. His agent's son took over, sold the agency to someone else. So on and so forth for 75 years. As he acquired assets, he stumbled into insurance policies. Not one single person attempted to bundle him for 75 years. I was the first.

Did they receive a Rate Increase?

Auto insurance costs rose 14.5% in February 2023, more than twice the rate of inflation (6%), making auto insurance account for a steadily increasing share of consumer discretionary spending. Accordingly, among those shopping for reasons of price, 44% say they are price checking and 42% say they are being spurred by a rate increase. Similarly, 41% of those shopping because of a rate increase say that their rate increased 20% or more (JD Power, 2023). Insurance is an 'inflation proof' business, rates always go up, at least in the long-term.

Poor Claim Experience

Claim satisfaction is an incredibly hard metric to track industry wide. However, it is a significant reporting factor for shopping and switching.

How often are people having Claims?

Do you ever wonder how often people actually have to use their insurance? Turns out, it's really not all that often. In 2022, 4.9 percent of collision insurance policyholders had a claim, while 3.3 percent of people with comprehensive coverage had a claim (Insurance Information Institute). And remember, many of those people are repeat users of insurance.

Poor Agent Experience

As a Former Insurance Agent, looking back at it, I'd say the vast majority of my clients came from shoppers who were dissatisfied with their Agent. In that same Insurance Shopper survey we referenced above, it found that among consumers who recently switched insurance *29% thought the reps were rude or had a negative approach.* There is a simple rule that I used to abide by, and that was to always throw the current agent under the bus, ethically of course.

I'll give you an example. I'm reviewing a Home Insurance Dec, and the Coverage A comes out to $155/SQFT in Los Angeles, CA. Now, I could attack that amount of coverage for being grossly under-insured. That'll more likely than not make the insured defensive and lose the spirit of collaboration in the sales conversation. So, how do I do that by throwing the current agent under the bus?

Agent: ~~You home is under-insured. You need more insurance. Because, blah, blah, blah...~~

Agent: John, looks like your home is only insured for $155 per SQFT. Can I ask... when was the last time your agent sat down with you and made sure your coverage was up to date to meet your current needs?

What do you figure that answer to that question is? I can tell you from personal experience, the answer **99% of the time** goes one of two ways.

Insured: Oh, I don't know. Twenty years ago, when I first signed up.

Insured: Never.

You can try convincing people they are under-insured until you get blue in the face, or you can ask a series of simple questions. I'm not going to tell them how to think, or what to think, I want to give them something interesting to think about. The point is, we change the conversation from Price to Value, but we have to fundamentally care about protecting the person.

Poor Insurance Company Experience

If someone has a poor experience, do you think they care more about having a better experience or saving money? Let's walk through the example below. According to a recent survey conducted by TechSee, *"The data shows that 39% of Americans who canceled a contract with a company in the previous 24 months cited customer service as the primary reason for cancellation."*

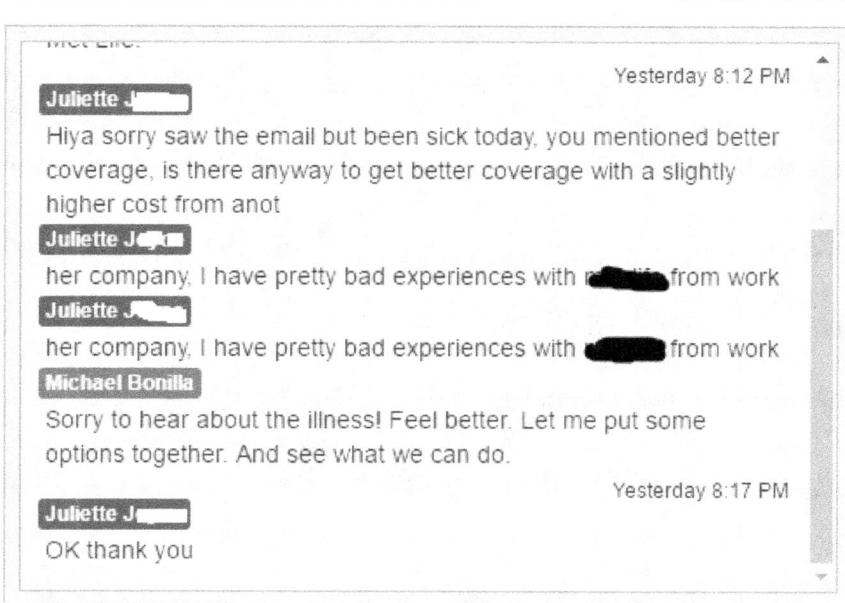

The above chat was a text log from a prospect email I sent

out. It was a simple proposition, "Would you consider paying

slightly more for your insurance if you could get better protection?"

Now, you only get three answers to that question; yes, no or it

depends. In the case of Juliette, she had a poor experience with her

insurance company and reached out to my email. She had a classic

case of 'no-one-ever-explained-my-policy-to-me-ever'. After a

single conversation, we signed her up for a considerably better

insurance policy at a higher cost. People will pay more for

insurance, if you give me a good reason to do so.

What Prompts a Consumer to Switch?

I have a controversial take, what prompts someone to shop might be different from the actual reason they choose to purchase insurance elsewhere. The difference between the number of consumers who left their insurance providers and those who are planning to leave is 6.9% (CallMiner Churn Index, 2022).

Problem Identification: Define the Problem

Problem Identification is the Turkey on Thanksgiving and customizing a solution is the gravy. Why do consumers talk to insurance agents? Because, they have a problem and think you might be able to solve it. If we can agree that most people are moderately insurance illiterate, then what are the odds they understand the breadth of their problems? The odds are rather low. Ultimately, our job is to solve problems.

Homeowners Underinsurance

Do people carry enough Homeowners Insurance? On average, do you think people are properly insured? I can tell you after reviewing thousands of Dec Pages, that people are more often than not, not properly insured. Don't take my word for it, let's look at objective data. According to Insurance Business America, **80 percent of homes affected by 2018 California wildfires were underinsured. For perspective, in the 2018 Wildfires there were approximately 18,000 Residences damaged or destroyed**. That's approximately, 16,000 underinsured properties from one peril, in one state, in one year.

From a National perspective, we see similar trends with under-insurance. According to Nationwide, "*The average underinsurance amount is about 22%, though some homes are underinsured by 60% or more.*" This shows that, 1 out 5 potential customers you speak with are grossly under-insured. And, odds are, they have no idea.

A new **American Property Casualty Insurance Association** (APCIA) survey of over 1,000 U.S. homeowners who have a homeowners insurance policy, reveals a majority of insured homeowners have not taken important steps to ensure their insurance coverage is keeping pace with rising inflation and increased building costs, which could leave policyholders underinsured if catastrophe strikes.

Under-insurance most likely happens in one of two ways. It happens at New Business, when the competing Agent copies the identical amount of incorrect insurance and then proceeds to sell that Amount of Insurance to the customer. It could also happen at Renewal, when the Agent fails to re-evaluate the Replacement Cost or check for upgrades, updates, or improvements. Ultimately, the root cause of the problem is education, care and commitment.

Automobile Underinsurance and Uninsured Motorist

When I first started in the insurance industry, I had no clue how many people driving around me didn't have insurance. In fact, some estimates put the Uninsured Driver Rates By State Range from 3% to 29% (Moneygeek.com). Imagine, 29% of the Drivers on the road not carrying any insurance. In 2019, 12.6 percent of motorists, or about one in eight drivers, were uninsured, according to a study by the Insurance Research Council (IRC).

Using non-wonky language

During the licensing process we learn all of these cools words, like, "Indemnification" or "Full Coverage"… It's important to remember, as we discussed above, most consumers **DO NOT UNDERTSAND** what in the world you are talking about. We live and breathe this stuff, but consumers look at it by-in-large as a necessary evil. Avoid 'wonky' language at all cost.

The term "Full Coverage" is probably the best example of the worst used phrase. What does it mean? It means nothing, yet it can mean literally everything is covered. Full Coverage should mean, you have purchased both Liability and Physical Damage coverage. As a term, it is really mis-used, because it is kind of just a made-up term. If you ask ten agents, and ten customers, what does "Full Coverage" mean to you, they might give you twenty different answers. If you ask an Error's and Omissions Attorney to define 'full coverage', they will simply answer, "Job Security."

Don't *Just* Stick the Turkey In the Oven

Have you ever cooked a Turkey? Would you want to eat a turkey that wasn't cooked properly? Or how about a Turkey that someone didn't check the temperature on? Or a Turkey that wasn't braised? What about a turkey that was taken right out of the freezer and stuck into the oven? What if the oven wasn't pre-heated to the correct temperature? What if the turkey wasn't cooked long enough? What if the turkey wasn't de-thawed? Even if you haven't cooked a turkey before in your entire life, does any of that sound right to you?

There is a correct process for cooking a turkey. After its cooked, do you just take it out and give it to people? No! You let it rest, and then you slice it to serve. Most Insurance Agents, take a frozen turkey right out the freezer and just shove it in the oven and slam it on the dining table.

Don't Open the Refrigerator without Asking for Permission First

There's an old saying that you should never go into another person's house and open their refrigerator without asking for permission first. It's considered to be rude. When asking for something, ask for permission to ask for something.

Agent: Would you be okay if we spent the next ten or fifteen minutes discussing how your insurance is supposed to work on your behalf? *(Why? Because, maybe they don't want to.)*

Everyone has a plan until they get punched in the mouth. – Mike Tyson

Defining a Sales Process Framework

Someone once told me to write down my sales process. At the time, I couldn't. He then told me that people who couldn't write down their process didn't know what they were doing. To which I told him, I know exactly what I am doing, I'm winging it! Let's outline the framework for a sales process.

Opening

What's your favorite Book? Aside from the one you're reading right now. What's your favorite Movie? In either case, do you remember the opening? Was the beginning of the movie memorable? Every great book, or movie, has an incredible opening that hooks you into the story. So, how do we do that with selling? We go back to the "Rational Decision-Making Process", start with defining a problem.

Setting the Table

Imagine two Thanksgiving Dinner tables. Table 1 has a long oak table, covered with a cloth, silverware, fine China, folded napkins, and at the center of the table a warm turkey. Table 2 is made of industrial plastic, it folds, one of the legs wobbles, there's a cheap plastic table cloth left over from a birthday party. There's a burnt turkey at the center, and nothing else. Food is a lot like selling, presentation makes a difference. When you open a sales conversation, you need to set expectations for the client. What should they expect from me and what I should expect from them. Most Agents rush into the underwriting conversation and skip the 'pre-heating' of the oven. You don't stick the turkey into the oven until the oven is at the proper temperature!

Consistency beats Talent

Research shows that most people make a first impression of a person within 7 seconds. You have seven seconds... what do you say?

Agent: What brings you by today?

Agent: How can we help?

Agent: What seems to be concerning you about your current insurance program?

Agent: Thanks for stopping by, what's on your mind?

Agent: Before we get started what kind of questions and concerns do you have?

Now... how can insured answer one of these three questions? Any way they want, because they are open-ended questions. Open-ended questions don't force the insured into a corner, which means they are less likely to get defensive or become entrenched into a position they cannot retreat from later on in the conversation.

How did they answer the question? Let us assume, they used the **P** word. What do you do?

Agent: What brings you by today?

Insured: I'm looking for a lower price.

So, you made it past the first 7 seconds. How do you make it past the 8th?

Agent: What brings you by today?

Insured: I'm looking for a lower price.

Agent: ~~Okay… I'm desperate… let me quote you my lowest price regardless the position it might put your family's financial future into someday.~~

Agent: ~~Great! I'm the cheapest guy on the block.~~

Agent: ~~If you're looking for the lowest price, you should check out DirectCaptiveInsurance.com. They don't use agents, and they are cheaper.~~ *(I'm putting this one in here, because an agent actually told me this during a secret shop.)*

What would you say in this situation? After working with thousands of insurance professionals, I can tell you what most people do... they fold, flop or flinch. People can pick up on your desperation. Consumers are built with defensive mechanisms against salespeople. Its human nature. Don't fight it, own it. One of the most important lessons you can learn is that you should be prepared to **respond to a situation, don't react**. If you have to react, you haven't practiced enough or prepared enough for the situation.

The worst mistake you can make in a sales conversation is trying to convince someone else you are right and they are wrong. If someone brings up a concern to you, don't avoid it, accept it and move on. How good does it feel to have your concerns acknowledged by another person? It sure feels a lot better than someone questioning my concerns. We know that most people think of price, most salespeople tend to lead with price, so how do we build a response around the inevitable **P** word?

Agent: What brings you by today?

Insured Scenario #1: I'm looking for a lower price.

Agent: I can appreciate that. Insurance rates are on the rise. Aside from Price, what else is important to you about your insurance?

Insured Scenario #2: I think I'm overpaying for my insurance.

Agent: ~~No you're not.~~

Agent: That's fair. Rates are on the rise. (**Be the first to agree. Validate, don't argue.**) What helps me sleep well at night is knowing that I protected your family, and your assets. I'm more than okay saying, "If you want someone to protect your family. I'm your insurance guy." I tend not to talk about the price very often. Granted, I recognize that price is part of our decision-making process for nearly everything we buy. The way I look at it, there's no such thing as a good deal for the wrong insurance policy. The most important part of your insurance, is that, if you need to use it, it's there for you to use. (Pause)

Agent: First and foremost, everything comes down to your coverage. If you need Insurance because your Home burns to the ground. It matters down to the penny what we put on that policy. If someone tries to embroil you in a lawsuit, then you'll see how an insurance policy actually works. Unfortunately, what most people don't realize is that even though they have insurance, they are at personal financial risk. Even though you're paying premium every month, you could still be personally on the hook for an accident.

Setting Expectations for the Call

It's important to let people know what to expect during your sales conversation. People hate surprises. The person is obviously expecting you do something in the conversation, and that is solve their problem. They don't know what kind of questions you might ask. They don't know how long the conversation might take. They don't know what they don't know. So, wouldn't it be important to let them know these things? I think so!

Agent: Today, really, I just have a few quick questions and then I'll hand it over to you to see if you have any questions for me. (Pause) Other than that I'll take the information that I have and put together a proposal for you and see if we can help you out. (Pause)

Insured: Sounds good.

Agent: Now, before we get started, do you have any questions, concerns or issues with your current insurance policy? *(This is a close ended question that looks like an open-ended question. But, it allows me to understand very quickly what the perception of the problem is for the customer.)*

Agent: How'd you hear about my Agency? *(A question that often gets overlooked, but also very important. Why is this SO important? According to the Independent Insurance Agents of Dallas. "A referred customer has an average 92% retention rate over the first 3 years versus a 67% retention rate for a customer from any other marketing source.")*

Insured: I told one of my friends, Bob, that I was looking for insurance and he referred me to you.

Agent: Have you just started looking? How far along are you in the shopping process? *(Why would I ask a question like this? Because, I want to know if I'm the First Agent, or Fifteenth Agent she's spoken with. Why do I want to know that? Well, I may not want a client who shops 15 agents on their renewal. This also gives us a strategic advantage to carve out our value and monopolize the shopping process. On average, people take one hour or less doing research and purchasing Auto or Home insurance. If I can ethically monopolize that one hour, then that will increase the odds of success.)*

Insured: Umm.. You're the first person I've called.

Agent: Well, in my humble opinion I think you called the right person first. Here's what I mean by that. We take a tremendous amount of pride in our process, and it is a bit detailed. As **we're** working together and going through that process, you'll probably say wow, I did call the right person first and that is a good bit of detail. But, don't worry. It really doesn't take all that long and I'll make sure to hold your hand every step of the way and do all the heavy lifting. See… What I've found by doing that, is that it makes the entire insurance buying process a much more comfortable experience.

Agent: Here's my process in a nutshell. Firstly, and most important. We're going to sit down and spend the time to educate you on how your insurance is supposed to work on your behalf. That way you know what it is that you are actually purchasing. Then we are going to customize the coverage to fit your specific needs and budget. Most people, as I walk through the process, they end up saying, "This insurance thing, it really isn't all that complicated or confusing as it has to be."

Agent: By the end of the process, whether you sign up with my agency or not. I want you to feel secure. If someday you actually need to use that insurance policy, years from now, and I get that 4 AM phone call. You're not going to have to question whether or not your covered. If a wildfire rips through your cul-de-sac, or your car jolts unexpectedly into an intersection, or someone gets injured on your property and sues you. When you call me up and report a claim, the first question out of my mouth, **AS YOUR AGENT**, is always the same...."Are you okay?" Trust me, cars are a lot easier to fix than people.

Qualifying (Client Underwriting Subjective/Objective)

Somewhere in my process, throughout the entire process really, I want to identify key buying behaviors. I want to flush out Belief Systems. Some people believe insurance is meant to be used. Some people believe insurance is meant to be used only in important situations. I want to get at the root of the person and find out from their perspective – what is insurance for? What does it mean for you to own insurance? When do you plan on using it? Have you used it in the past? How do you think of insurance as a product? What's the polite way of asking someone if they've had a claim?

Agent: Have you ever had to use your insurance before?

Agent: Would you consider paying slightly more for better coverage?

Agent: Would you consider paying slightly more if I could bundle all of your policies with a single company?

Agent: Would you ever consider paying slightly more for insurance that better protects your family?

Needs Analysis (Field Underwriting Objective)

Underwriting questions are critically important in a sales conversation. Most carriers help speed this up with Prior Carrier Reporting, Vehicle LookUp, MVR/CLUE and easily accessible Aerial Photos.

- How much Insurance does this person need?

- How much Insurance can I find for them?

- What are they willing to insure?

- What are they not willing to insure?

- What is too much insurance?

- What is not enough insurance?

- What do they need?

- What do they want?

- How do they like to pay?

- When do they like to pay?

Do they want coverage for a Wedding Ring? (Personal Article Floater Example)

Agent: Mrs. Prospect, I noticed that your current Agent isn't protecting your Wedding ring. Can I ask why that is?

Insured: I had no idea it wasn't protected.

Agent: Is that something you want coverage for?

Insured: How much does something like that cost? (Buying Question)

Agent: On average, about $8 per month... (Pause)

I can't tell you how many policies I won from other agents, using that very short sales pitch. Adding a Personal Article Floater onto most Home Insurance policies is somewhere in the ballpark of $8 per month. It's one of the easiest up-sell tactics you can use when selling insurance.

How often do you see Wedding Ring Endorsements on Home or Renters Insurance? Maybe 5% of the time an agent bothered to Endorse it, and let's say 5% of clients buy a standalone policy. We know that 55% of people Own a Home and 55% of people more or less are married. That means somewhere around 50% of people don't have coverage beyond the Sublimit for Jewelry built into an Insurance contract. That is a massive gap in coverage that is incredibly easy to demonstrate to a prospect.

Earthquake Cross-Sell/Transition

According to the California Department of Insurance, approximately *12.71%* of the Residential market are currently protected from Earthquakes. In the state with the most frequent and severe earthquakes have any protection against earthquakes.

Agent: Mr. Prospect, I noticed your current Agent isn't protecting your Homes' Equity against Earthquakes. Can I ask why *they* chose to do that?

Agent: By the way Mr. Prospect, who is your current earthquake Insurance through?

Flood Insurance

According to USA Today, <u>only 2% of homeowners in California have flood insurance</u>. That is a rather worrisome number when you consider that approximately 1.4M Californians live in a Special Flood Hazard Area. I have conducted hundreds of secret shops, if not thousands at this point, and not one agent has offered me either an Earthquake Quote or Flood Quote. Flood insurance costs an average of $859 a year from the NFIP. An NFIP policy provides up to $250,000 of dwelling coverage and $100,000 for contents coverage. This is massive gap to fill...

Bodily Injury Protection

Agent: I'm a little worried about your Bodily Injury Limits. Do you feel you have enough protection? What I mean is, do you feel you have enough coverage to protect you against major claims? (This is a close-ended question. This questions helps me gauge if someone cares or not about protecting their stuff. The inherit risk you run when asking a close-ended question is that the person answers the wrong way and shuts down the conversation. This is what is called a potential 'point of failure' in a process.)

> **Insured:** Yes. I have plenty of coverage.

~~**Agent:** No you don't.~~

~~**Agent:** Are you sure???~~

Agent: Currently, you have $15,000/$30,000 in Bodily Injury protection. How did your Agent determine that was enough coverage to protect ALL of your assets. *(You see how a close-ended question can paint you into a corner? It can very easily drag down the conversation)*

Note: Not everyone is going to want what you offer. One thing I did in these situations was provide a "Assets Exposed Acknowledgment" form. The form simply stated the current limits of liability, the average Jury Award for a Personal Injury Lawsuit in California and a statement 'waiving the right to sue the agent in the case they do not have enough insurance'. This tended to convince most people to just buy the higher limits of liability. Some people need to see it spelled out in black-and-white.

Homeowners Liability Protection

How often do you run into Dec pages with $100,000 liability? I can never understand it. Is your home worth less than $100,000? Is your equity in the home less than $100,000? What about your stuff that can get repossessed?

Agent: ~~You should get more liability protection in case you get sued.~~

Agent: I noticed that your Liability Protection is only $100,000. Can I ask why your agent did that?

Agent: I'm worried about your liability coverage. Do you feel you have enough coverage to protect your Home's equity?

Agent: Have you ever considered purchasing better liability protection?

Agent: Have you ever thought about buying better insurance protection?

Agent: Would you ever consider buying better protection for your families assets?

Forecasting and Foreshadowing

Agent: Here are the next steps. I'll take this info and generate a proposal based off some of things you said and we'll set up some time to go over the proposal. By the time were done, you will know your secure, safe and what **IT IS** you are actually purchasing. When we put that proposal together, what I hope you'll feel is that, when I make a coverage recommendation. You'll know exactly why I made that recommendation.

Agent: Would you like to go over the proposal at your home or at my office? *(As a rule of thumb, I made this offer to any prospect within 25 miles of my office. Times have changed, but if you still have an office, why not ask? You never know.)*

Qualifying a Client

My Grandmother recently relocated to California from Virginia, and she never handled the insurance prior to my Grandfather passing away. This is the unfortunate reality with many widows. They get an experience as to what they don't know very quickly. When she relocated to California, I referred her to a local agency for help. They sold her a policy, and I assumed she was taken care of. Little did I know, they didn't have a coverage conversation with her. They sold her the coverage, but they never explained how it worked, repeating the cycle of insurance illiteracy. My Grandmother asked me to come over and sit down at her kitchen table and 'go through her insurance'.

The first question I asked my Grandmother, was the first question I asked every client in the Qualifying stage. My grandmother was 75 at the time, and I asked her, *"Has anyone ever bothered to sit down with you and explain how your insurance is supposed to work on your behalf?"* The answer, was No. The answer from my experience is almost always is No. Sometimes, the answer is 'Twenty Years Ago, when I first signed up..."

Hypothetical Qualifying Conversation

Agent: ~~Start talking about insurance.~~

Agent: Has anyone ever bothered to sit down and explain your coverage?

Agent: Has anyone ever spent the time with you to explain how your coverage is supposed to work on your behalf?

Agent: When was the last time anyone sat down and explained your coverage to you?

Agent: When was the last time your agent spent the time to explain your coverage and make sure it was up to date?

Mr. Prospect: Never.

Agent: ~~Let me tell you all about insurance...~~

Agent: Would you mind if we spent *five* or *ten* minutes discussing it?

How do you qualify a client?

How do you know when a client is a good fit for your agency? How do you know that you are a good fit for the client? When do you know 'when' to write a policy? When do you know 'when' not to write a policy?

Presentation

The Presentation is the Solution to the Problem. It's important to re-emphasis the problems that were identified earlier and amplify how your solution solves those specific problems. This is where you can really sell your value as an agent and explain the coverage. This is where you can make your Professional Recommendation. Or, you can just present a price. We're not going to go through an entire Presentation, just some high points I think are worth talking about.

Opening a Presentation Conversation

Agent: Thanks for carving out the time to meet with me. I think we put together a great proposal for you, based on everything we discussed last time. Blah Blah Blah. (Insert some Rapport stuff) Luckily, based on your excellent driving record and insurance history. I was able to qualify you for my best insurance company. Did any questions pop-up or did you have any outstanding concerns?

Agent: No? Great! There's a lot to unpack here. But, I'll make sure to do all of the heavy lifting and answer any questions that will probably come up.

Agent: The first question I have for you, (When was) Has anyone actually bothered to sit down with you and explain how your insurance works?

> **Insured:** No.

> **Insured:** When I signed up twenty years ago... Maybe...

Agent: No worries. One of the key benefits of being with my agency is that we focus on education. Would you be okay with us spending a few minutes to go over how your insurance works?

> **Insured:** Yes, please.

Establishing Your Value (Foreshadowing)

Somewhere in the conversation I want to foreshadow the purpose of insurance. What is the purpose of insurance? It's to make you whole again, after a covered loss. But, how do we make that relatable to an insured?

Water-Back Up Sewer and Drainage

Agent: John, I noticed that your current policy wasn't covering you in the event of a Sewer Back up. Have you ever thought about adding that coverage on to your policy?

Insured: No idea what you're talking about.

Agent: You ever go on vacation?

Insured: Sure.

Agent: You ever drive up the California coast? We like to go to Cambria from Thousand Oaks.

Insured: Sure. We go up the Central coast once a year.

Agent: Me too. Let's say I'm driving up the coastline, going away for a weekend to Cambria. It's a three-hour drive from our house. I made sure to shut the air off. Something happens in my house right after I leave. It rains. And, oh boy, does it rain. It rains all the way up. All three hours. In my house though, something is happening. My toilet starts to bubble... and bubble... and bubble... Little do I know, I'm three hours up the coast already. Sewage starts spewing out of my toilet and overflowing... everywhere...

Mind you, I'm up in Cambria having the time of my life. Friday night rolls around, sewage is spewing. Saturday rolls around, sewage spewing. Sunday rolls around and I make the trek back down to Thousand Oaks. I get out, stretch my legs. Put the key in the door. As I turn the key and open the door, hoping to see my home. I'm hit with the worst stench of my life, the most grotesque odor I have ever smelt. Because, for the past 72 hours, Raw sewage was fermenting in my home. It's on the walls. It's on the ceiling somehow. It's on the towels. It's in the bathtub. It's all over the floor. It's on the family photo albums. It's everywhere. And, for the past 72 hours I had no air circulating in the house. And you know what the worst part of these claims are?

Insured: No idea. The sewage?

Agent: The fact you can't live in your own home without dry heaving, and for who knows how long until the odor is finally gone. Is that something you want coverage for?

Making a Home Insurance Deductible Relatable

A Sales Tactic I designed my entire sales process around was Premium Arbitrage. I would use the reality of the insurance market place, most people are under-insured and rarely use their insurance. Both of these facts we know to be true. Deductibles as a matter of fact acted as the conduit to buying down additional insurance by lowering the premium. What do I mean by that? I mean that with a higher deductible, you get a lower premium and that builds room to buy more coverage. There's a reason why insurance companies give a reduced premium for a higher deductible. Higher deductibles reduce moral hazard, they reduce fraudulent claim potential and they tell us how the client views insurance. At what level the client is willing to involve their insurance or choose to self-insure a loss.

Agent: ~~We recommend a higher deductible because you'll save money.~~

Agent: ~~We recommend a higher deductible because insurance is not for the small things it's for the big things.~~

Agent: ~~You should go with a higher deductible because you don't want to file small claims anyway.~~

Agent: Mr. Prospect, I noticed your home insurance deductible was $500. Can I ask why?

> Mr. Prospect: I've kind of always had it $500.

Agent: Have you ever considered increasing it?

> Mr. Prospect: No.

Agent: ~~Why not? Why didn't you? Why would you do that?~~ *(Many Agents are trained to ask 'why' a lot during their sales process, but that can make the conversation confrontational and not collaborative. Being inquisitive is an incredibly powerful skillset when selling, but you have to know when to be inquisitive and determine what beneficial piece of information will you receive from asking a question. Asking questions for the sake of asking questions can turn a sales conversation into a sales interrogation.)*

Agent: ~~If you increase your deductible you can save X amount.~~

Agent: Let ask you something, Mr. Prospect, have you ever had to actually use your insurance before?

Mr. Prospect: No.

Agent: Well, do you plan on using it any time soon?

Mr. Prospect: No.

Agent: If your home were to burn to the ground, do you think you could find $5000 to rebuild it?

Agent: What's the smallest claim you'd want to get your insurance involved?

Agent: You look pretty handy, do you think you'd even get your insurance involved for less than $5000?

Agent: If you consider increasing your Deductible from $500, to $5000, you'd be able to save about 40% on your Home Insurance. Is that something you'd be interested in?

Scenario: Homeowner is Underinsured by 20% or more.

Let's say you get a Dec Page showing Coverage A at $150 per SQFT. What do you do to convince the person to pay the correct amount for insurance? Now savings money is not even in the question. A home in California needs about $300/SQFT to build from ground up construction. Keep in mind there is theoretical cushion for Extended Replacement Cost. We know most people are under-insured in California and across the United States. So, what do we do?

Agent: ~~You need more insurance...~~

~~Agent: You are under-insured...~~

Agent: I'm a little worried about the amount of insurance protecting your home. Have you ever considered increasing it?

Agent: Do you know when the last time your agent made sure your home policy was up to date?

Agent: Do you know when the last time your agent made sure your policy had enough coverage?

Agent: When was the last time your agent sat down to make sure your coverage was enough to currently meet your needs?

Insured: Twenty Years Ago.

Agent: Do you think the value of your home has gone down or up in the past Twenty Years?

Insured: Way up!

Agent: Would you like your insurance to reflect the value Twenty Years Ago, or what it might take to replace it in today's dollars?

Personal Auto Policy

Scenario: Bodily Injury Limits do not Match UMBI Limits

This scenario was always the most perplexing situation I ever ran into, yet for some reason in California it is all too common. What kind of client would knowingly agree to higher Bodily Injury than UMBI? Your agent is willing to give a Third Party more money, than you would expect to get if injured from an accident.

Agent: I noticed that your current Agent decided to not match your Bodily Injury with Uninsured Motorist Bodily Injury. Did he explain why?

Insured: I have no idea.

Agent: Well, are you okay with potentially giving someone else $100,000, but if you are injured by an uninsured motorist you only getting up to $15,000? Basically, what your agent did was set up a policy to give someone else more money than you would want to receive if in the reverse situation. Would you like me to match those limits?

Medical Payments Coverage Personal Auto

This Coverage gets stripped off of most Auto insurance policies in California, or is rarely ever sold at a meaningful amount of coverage. The ironic part is that Med Pay is not only a typically profitable coverage to sell, but is very inexpensive for the most part.

Agent: John, I noticed that your current Agent isn't protecting your family with Medical Payment coverage. Can I ask why?

Agent: John, have you ever thought about purchasing Medical Payment Coverage?

Agent: John, have you ever considered about buying Medical Payment Coverage?

Agent: John, I'm a little concerned that you might be exposed to paying Out-of-Pocket Costs from Accidents. Have you heard of Medical Payment coverage?

> Insured: What is that? He told me I don't need it.

Agent: Do you know if your current Health Insurance policy will cover an Ambulance ride if you get into an accident?

> Insured: I have no idea.

Agent: Me either. Here is what I know. X% of ambulance rides are out of pocket and the average cost in your area is $Y. As your Agent, I recommend we go with at least the average out-of-pocket cost. Is that something you want coverage for?

Closing

Closing the least understood part of selling. If a sales process was 100%, closing should be less than 1% of your overall process. Someone once told me, that to close, you ask a question and shut up. It's called a close because you are looking for a resolution, which means in general, you should use Close Ended questions. You want a Yes or a No.

Agent: How would you like to pay?

This is called the Assumptive Close. You are assuming they want to purchase. And, if I did my job correctly, they do. My mentor taught me a simple formula for closing. He said, "Present a Price. Ask a question. Shut up and wait for the answer." Have you ever heard the phrase, he who speaks first loses? The truth is, after you make a recommendation or ask a question, that is very true. Why is it true? Because, people can pick up on your energy. If you make a recommendation or answer your own question, please can sense a level of nervousness. Ask a question, shut up and wait for answer.

Conclusion

Buying Insurance doesn't have to be complicated. Buying Insurance doesn't have to be confusing. Buying Insurance doesn't have to be daunting. Neither does selling it. In summation, telling isn't selling. Questions are great, but they need to lead you somewhere productive. Don't ask a question you don't know the answer to. Don't be afraid to say, "I'll find out." Don't act too desperate. Selling is both an artform and a science. No sales process is perfect. Every sales process should change depending on the client. Every sales process should change overtime. Every sales process should adapt to the needs of the client. Every sales process should have flexibility. Every sales process should fit your specific way of speaking. No sales process is going to be a silver-bullet. No sales process will work every time. Selling is hard work. You are going to fail, often. Most of our job is getting rejected, which is what makes it challenging. It sure becomes a lot easier however, if we have a process.

Reference

Vorha, Tanveehn. "96% of American Drivers Don't Understand Their

    Car Insurance Policies." *Business Wire*, 28 Apr. 2022,

    www.businesswire.com/news/home/20220428005489/en/96

    -of-American-Drivers-Don%E2%80%99t-Understand-Their-

    Car-Insurance-

    Policies#:~:text=%2D%2096%25%20of%20drivers%20misunde

    rstand%20at,multiple%20features%20of%20their%20coverag

    e.

Spitznagel, Eric. "Why We Keep Seeing so Many Insurance Ads - as

    Beer Ads Have Disappeared." *New York Post*, New York Post,

    12 Feb. 2022, nypost.com/2022/02/12/why-were-seeing-

    more-insurance-ads-while-beer-ads-fade-out/.

Bazerman, M. H., & Moore, D. A. (2012). *Judgment in Managerial*

    Decision Making, 8th Edition. John Wiley & Sons.

Edwards, Vanessa Van. "The Ultimate Guide to Making a Great First

Impression (Even Online)." *Science of People*, 26 Oct. 2023,

www.scienceofpeople.com/first-impressions/.

*Nearly 15% of Consumers Allow Auto Insurance Coverage to Lapse

as Shopping Fails to Yield Lower Rates*, TransUnion, 15 May

2023, newsroom.transunion.com/nearly-15-of-consumers-

allow-auto-insurance-coverage-to-lapse--as-shopping-fails-to-

yield-lower-rates/.

www.kin.com. "Report: How Many Us Homes Are Underinsured?"

Kin Insurance, 2021, www.kin.com/blog/underinsurance-

report/#:~:text=According%20to%20Insurance%20Business%

20America,2018%20California%20wildfires%20were%20unde

rinsured.

"Underinsured Home Insurance FAQ." *Nationwide*, 2023,

www.nationwide.com/lc/resources/home/articles/underinsur

ance.

Insurance Journal. "Most Homeowners Underinsured for Trends in

Inflation, Building Costs: Apcia." *Insurance Journal*, 6 May

2022,

www.insurancejournal.com/news/national/2022/05/06/6664

06.htm.

"How Many Motorists in America Are Uninsured? Facts &

Statistics." *Moneygeek.Com*,

www.moneygeek.com/insurance/auto/resources/uninsured-

motorist-facts/. Accessed 13 Jan. 2024.

"Facts + Statistics: Uninsured Motorists." *III*, www.iii.org/fact-

statistic/facts-statistics-uninsured-motorists. Accessed 13 Jan.

2024.

California, State of. "Residential and Earthquake Insurance

Coverage Study." *CA Department of Insurance*, 2023,

www.insurance.ca.gov/0400-news/0200-studies-

reports/0300-earthquake-study/index.cfm.

Michael Jans, et al. "Why to Never Sell Based on Price." *Why to*

   Never Sell Based on Price | Insurance Thought Leadership, 13

   July 2016, www.insurancethoughtleadership.com/agent-

   broker/why-never-sell-based-price.

Churn in the insurance industry - survey report 2019. TechSee.

   (2022, December 31).

   https://techsee.me/resources/reports/2019-insurance-churn-

   survey/

The CallMiner churn index 2020 - assets.ctfassets.net. (n.d.).

   https://assets.ctfassets.net/xj0skx6m69u2/3a2jGBo5R1M1DO

   ZiWU7A8U/78b7a94de8851a5bbd68b9d01c230411/whitepap

   er-uk-callminer-churn-utilities.pdf

Thomas, L. (n.d.). AIA Dallas.

   https://www.iiadallas.org/page/75#:~:text=A%20referred%20

   first%2Dyear%20customer,from%20any%20other%20marketi

   ng%20source.

Rosonke, S. (2023, December 18). *3 simple ways to increase insurance client retention*. AgencyBloc Insurance Agency CRM. https://www.agencybloc.com/ams/customer-and-policy-management/insurance-crm/how-to-increase-client-retention/

agentero. (n.d.). *The latest insights and thought leadership for independent insurance agents.* Agentero. https://blog.agentero.com/post/how-to-retain-customers-in-the-insurance-industry

MICHAEL BONILLA, CPCU, ARM

NEVER $ELL ON PRICE

An Insurance Agent Guidebook to developing a Consultative Sales Process for Auto and Home Insurance.